# Buddhism And The 32 Characteristics Of A Great Man

Henry Alabaster

**Kessinger Publishing's Rare Reprints**

**Thousands of Scarce and Hard-to-Find Books on These and other Subjects!**

- Americana
- Ancient Mysteries
- Animals
- Anthropology
- Architecture
- Arts
- Astrology
- Bibliographies
- Biographies & Memoirs
- Body, Mind & Spirit
- Business & Investing
- Children & Young Adult
- Collectibles
- Comparative Religions
- Crafts & Hobbies
- Earth Sciences
- Education
- Ephemera
- Fiction
- Folklore
- Geography
- Health & Diet
- History
- Hobbies & Leisure
- Humor
- Illustrated Books
- Language & Culture
- Law
- Life Sciences
- Literature
- Medicine & Pharmacy
- Metaphysical
- Music
- Mystery & Crime
- Mythology
- Natural History
- Outdoor & Nature
- Philosophy
- Poetry
- Political Science
- Science
- Psychiatry & Psychology
- Reference
- Religion & Spiritualism
- Rhetoric
- Sacred Books
- Science Fiction
- Science & Technology
- Self-Help
- Social Sciences
- Symbolism
- Theatre & Drama
- Theology
- Travel & Explorations
- War & Military
- Women
- Yoga
- *Plus Much More!*

**We kindly invite you to view our catalog list at: http://www.kessinger.net**

THIS ARTICLE WAS EXTRACTED FROM THE BOOK:

Wheel of the Law

BY THIS AUTHOR:

Henry Alabaster

ISBN 0766104265

READ MORE ABOUT THE BOOK AT OUR WEB SITE:

http://www.kessinger.net

OR ORDER THE COMPLETE
BOOK FROM YOUR FAVORITE STORE

ISBN 0766104265

Because this article has been extracted from a parent book, it may have non-pertinent text at the beginning or end of it.

# APPENDIX.

---

## THE THIRTY-TWO CHARACTERISTICS OF A GREAT MAN.

In predicting the glorious future of the young Prince, born to be a Buddha, the Brahmin soothsayers, skilled in Vedic lore, relied on the appearance of the thirty-two principal, and eighty minor, characteristics of a great man; the marks which were a sure sign that their bearer would be either temporal or spiritual Lord of the whole world, that is, either a Chakkravartin Emperor, ruler over all the continents, or a Buddha, teacher of all beings.

According to the Siamese account, Brahma had previously descended from heaven, and appeared in human form, merely to teach men the signs by which they might recognise the Great Being who would be born for their salvation.

These signs probably are the various characteristics ascribed to or possessed by different Indian heroes, and exaggerated by the fancies of Indian poets; and we may suppose that they have been formulated in a list, as "the thirty-two great signs" for at least twenty-two centuries.

M. Burnouf, in an appendix to the "Lotus de la bonne Loi," treats of these signs almost exhaustively. They interested him under two aspects—one as illustrating the authenticity of Buddhist classics, evidenced by the concurrence of the records of the Northern and Southern Buddhists, the other in connection with a theory that they showed the race to which Buddha belonged—certain persons having, on account of the curled hairs described in the list, and shown in idols, supposed Buddha to have been a negro.

The list has lost its interest in connection with these points; no one now supposes Buddha to have been a negro, and the age of Buddhist books is established by something better than the similarity of the lists contained in Northern and Southern records.

The concurrence of these lists only carries us back to the beginning of the fifth century; for Buddhaghosha, the commentator and translator into Pali of the Singhalese sacred works, learned his Pali in India, and would naturally have made the lists in his translations agree with the Indian lists, which he must have learned.

We have in the sculptures of the Sanchi Tope a better proof of the antiquity of Buddhist records than any afforded by comparison of Northern and Southern books, for these sculptures are evident illustrations of stories contained in the books, and it is manifest that the age of a story must be greater than that of its illustrations. The researches of scholars in China have also given us some valuable dates, considerably anterior to the days of Buddhaghosha.*

I will now quote the list as given by Burnouf:—

1. His head is crowned with a protuberance of the skull.
2. His curly hair is of a brilliant black, shining like the tail of a peacock, or sparkling collyrium (eye-salve), and each curl turns from left to right.
3. He has a broad and regular forehead.
4. Between his eyebrows is a circle of down, brilliant as snow or silver.
5. His eyelids are like those of a heifer.
6. He has brilliant black eyes.

* See Introduction to the Rev. S. Beal's "Travels of Buddhist Pilgrims."

7, 8, 9. He has forty teeth, all equal, set closely together, and of the most perfect whiteness.
10. His voice is like that of Brahma.
11. He has an exquisite sense of taste.
12. His tongue is broad and thin, or, according to the Thibetan version, "long and thread-like."
13. He has the jaw of a lion.
14. His shoulders or arms are perfectly rounded.
15. He has seven parts of his body filled out, or with protuberances (*i.e.*, soles of feet, palms of hands, shoulders, and back).
16. The space between his shoulders is covered.
17. His skin has the lustre or colour of gold.
18. His arms are so long that when he stands upright his hands reach to his knees.
19. His front is lion-like.
20. His body is perfectly straight, tall as a banyan-tree, and round in proportion.
21. His hairs grow one by one.
22. And their ends are turned to the right.
23. The generative organs are concealed.
24, 25. He has perfectly round thighs, and his legs are like those of the King of the Gazelles.
26. His toes or fingers are long.
27. The nails of the toes are well developed.
28. His instep is high.
29. His feet and hands are soft and delicate.
30. His toes and fingers are marked with lines forming a network.
31. Under the soles of his feet are marked two beautiful, luminous, brilliant white wheels, with a thousand rays.
32. His feet are even and well placed.

Such is the list given by M. Burnouf. In the fourth chapter of the "Life of Buddha" is the Siamese list. The differences between the two are very trifling. Scarcely one character of importance is wanting in the Siamese list, and the only additions of consequence are four large canine teeth (which M. Burnouf places among the eighty secondary signs), and a peculiar attachment of the feet to the body—such that, while they remained still, the whole body could move round on them as on a pivot.

CPSIA information can be obtained
at www.ICGtesting.com
Printed in the USA
LVIC06n1825071216
516243LV00023B/197